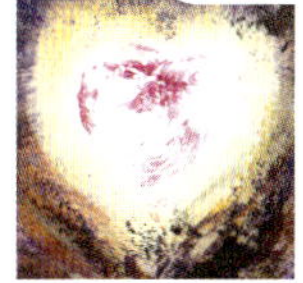

Opening the Heart

REFLECTIONS, PRACTICES AND **PRAYERS** TO GUIDE US TOWARD BEAUTY AND GRATITUDE

Kathy Hendricks

TWENTY-THIRD PUBLICATIONS
twentythirdpublications.com

Twenty-Third Publications
977 Hartford Turnpike Unit A
Waterford, CT 06385
(860) 437-3012 or (800) 321-0411
twentythirdpublications.com

IMAGE CREDITS:

Cover photo: © Ron Hendricks. Used with permission.

page 3, Stained Glass © jorisvo/stock.adobe.com

page 13, *Lily Pads* © Ron Hendricks. Used with permission.

page 14, *Ice and Rock* © Ron Hendricks 2011. Used with permission.

page 26, *Sacred Heart* © Linda McCray 2013. Used with permission.

page 31, Sacred Heart of Jesus © Maria Rattà/stock.adobe.com

page 40, *Our Lady of Sorrows* © William Hart McNichols.
www.FrBillMcNichols-SacredImages.com. Used with permission.

page 58, *Beauty Unfolding* © Ron Hendricks 2008. Used with permission.

ISBN: 978-1-62785-867-0
Printed in the U.S.A.

This absolutely beautiful book invites us to meditate on the place of the heart in our lives—the heart as it appears in the Bible, Jesus' sacred heart, Mary's immaculate heart, the very heart of God—to help us to love more and love more deeply. Hendricks's book correctly diagnoses a certain "heart dis-ease" in the world, a meanness that has taken hold in too many places in our world. Her new book, then, is a warm and inviting antidote to that kind of spreading dis-ease. *Cor ad cor loquitur* goes the motto of St. John Henry Newman, that is, "Heart speaks to heart." This book will speak to, and enlarge, your own heart, and in the process help you share the love that God intends for you to share, with a world desperately in need of that love.

JAMES MARTIN, SJ, *author of* ***Learning to Pray***

In *Opening the Heart*, Kathy Hendricks has created a masterful work of literary art. There are countless reasons to read it, savor it, and allow its contents to assist us as we strive to "conform our hearts to the heart of Christ." In these pages she harnesses the power of Scripture, spiritual insight, and storytelling to provide for us a road map for resisting and even reversing what she describes as "an alarming decline in empathy in our world."

Opening the Heart is uniquely designed to address the chaos and confusion of this challenging time in our history. With powerful pastoral words of care and concern it provides reasons for hoping and strategies for loving all of God's creation. Our nation and our world can only be healed by a return to civility, compassion, and hearts open to love. This excellent resource will help us complete that journey.

WILLIAM B. MILLER, *retreat leader, spiritual director, and author of* ***A Time of Blessings and Peace***

In her engaging style, Hendricks weaves together stories, Scripture, poetry, prayers, and wisdom from a variety of authors both ancient and contemporary. By focusing on the health of our spiritual hearts, Hendricks offers positive and inspiring ways for our hearts to become more open and whole. She addresses timely topics such as empathy deficit, holy longings, courage, joy, mysticism, and suffering as "a gateway into unity with others." Her reflective questions provide the basis for personal pondering as well as for group sharing. Deeply rooted in daily life, Hendricks's book is a rich source for expanding our capacity for love—not only love of God, but also love of others who walk our earthly journey with us.

SISTER MELANNIE SVOBODA, SND,
author of ***Sunflower Seeds of Hope***

Kathy Hendricks has gifted us with a profoundly moving book that takes us on a journey deep into the heart. We are free to explore, guided by Scripture, the mystical and contemplative traditions, philosophy, literature, and the author's own lived experiences. Each chapter is rich with insights that flow one upon another into a gently immersive wave of inspiration, understanding, and peace. If you've noticed some chaos, rigidity, or malaise creeping into your heart (and honestly, who hasn't?), this beautifully personal book can help you break free by adopting practices that nourish your own innate love, generosity, and sense of God's presence. I can't recommend this book enough—for small groups, individuals, and anyone feeling in need of some good heart work.

CONNIE CLARK, *author of* ***Called to Change the World***

FOR RON,

in gratitude for

the warmth of heart

you have shared with me

for fifty years.

CONTENTS

INTRODUCTION

Heart disease is the number one cause of death in the United States for both men and women. There are, however, preventative measures that can reduce the risks of coronary failure and subsequently improve one's quality of life.

Heart dis-ease might be approached in similar fashion. As with the physical heart, the spiritual heart needs safeguarding from perpetual anxiety, fear, anger, resentment, contempt, and cynicism. By opening our hearts to God's grace and love, we expand our capacity for mercy, compassion, empathy, joy, gratitude, hope, and other life-giving virtues. In hard-hearted times, it is all the more vital to remain alert to toxic elements that damage the inner heart and to adopt practices that keep it warm, tender, and pliable. The following chapters address both of these topics and offer insights, reflections, and inspiration into the way of the open heart.

It begins with the meaning of the heart in an emotional and spiritual sense and why it figures so predominantly in culture and in Scripture. We then move to causes for the hardened heart and how this affects us at both the personal and communal levels. The image and vision of the Sacred Heart of Jesus provide a powerful way of understanding what it means to replace a heart of stone with one of flesh. This, in turn, gives us a heart for others—exemplified by the Immaculate Heart of Mary and the expansion of empathy and compassion. Finally, we delve into the beauty of the contemplative heart and the love offered to us without reservation through God's expansive heart.

Our hearts do not beat in isolation but rather in tune with those of others. The generosity and care we receive from family, friends, colleagues, acquaintances, and chance encounters offer nourishment that makes our hearts grow. I write about some of my own experiences in a section called "Heart Warmers" at the end of each chapter. I hope this will prompt you to surface your own encounters. Space for you to write about them appears at the back of the book. There are also questions and suggested practices and actions that you can use for personal reflection or in discussion with others in your faith community, family, or book study group. Each chapter concludes with a prayer of reflection drawn from Ken Phillips' "A Meditation at the Feast of Saint Valentine." I am deeply grateful for his permission to use this beautiful prayer. A list of resources at the back of the book provides ideas for further reading about topics related to each chapter.

My hope is that you will find in this book inspiration that will ignite the flame in your own heart and enable you to cherish the light it provides for others. In such a way may our collective hearts join together in an offering of peace and kindness to a world that is in great need of it.

Kathy Hendricks

Opening *the* Heart

1

"VALENTINE HEARTS" BY RIVER GRACE WOELZ, AGE 7

The Heart's Meaning

With all vigilance guard your heart,
for in it are the sources of life.

PROVERBS 4:23

Have a heart
Cross my heart
Heartbeat
Coldhearted
Bless your heart
From the bottom of my heart
Broken-hearted
Eat your heart out
Half-hearted
Bleeding heart
At the heart of the matter
A heart of gold
Take heart
Wear your heart on your sleeve

These are just a few of the many idioms referring to the heart. They encompass everything from one's deepest desire to the desolation of loss, from sincerity to duplicity, from caring to indifference, from affection to cynicism. The meaning of the human heart goes way beyond a functional organ pumping blood through the body. How and why does the heart capture our imagination to such a degree that we have so many ways to speak of it?

Let us start with its shape. Due to its simplicity, a heart is one of the first things little children learn to draw. The origins of its iconic shape have been attributed to various plants, such as ivy, lily pads, and silphium, an ancient and now extinct species of giant fennel grown in Crete that produced heart-shaped seed pods. Used as part of decorative art, the shape took hold as a symbol of love and affection and reached widespread use as such during the Victorian era. While not identical to the shape of the human heart, the V-shaped image also became associated with emotions. Some ancient philosophers considered the heart to be the seat of the soul. Myth, art, literature, music, pop culture, and religion all added to an expanded view of the heart as representative of romantic, filial, and universal love. This is highly visible in the huge sales around Valentine's Day when, in 2023, sales of related products were estimated at $50 billion in both the U.S. and Canada.

The spirituality of the heart

The Bible contains over a thousand references to the heart—more than those for the body, the mind, or even the soul. Both the Hebrew and Christian Scriptures employ various descriptions of the heart's capacities. At its best, the heart is happy, peaceful, merry, clean, cheerful, and generous. At its worst, it is deceitful, cunning, and cold. In her book *Heart: A Natural History of the Heart-Filled Life*, Gail Godwin describes how the ancient Hebrews understood the heart—*lev*—as "the seat of wisdom and understanding, the inner personality, the whole gamut of emotional life, as well as the collective mind, or mind-set, of the people, the mental heart as well as the fleshy heart...." In the Gospel of Matthew, Jesus refers to the heart as the dwelling place of our deepest desires. "For where your treasure is, there also will your heart be" (Matthew 6:21).

This brings to mind another heart idiom: "What's in your heart?" In other words, what do you really intend, mean, feel, or desire? What do you treasure most? Such a reference moves beyond sentimental or romantic images of the heart to something deeper. Heart wisdom helps us discern whether something is authentic. To know something in the heart is to recognize that which is truly valuable and most profound. This makes the heart the site of our encounter with the Divine. In *The Awakened Heart*, psychologist and theologian Gerald May described it as "the place where we are in most intimate contact with God's presence and with our essential union with others, where the deep, ongoing love affair between God and human beings actually takes place." Accessing this sacred place requires attentiveness and spiritual discipline.

It is common to separate this notion of the heart from the head. Doing so makes the heart purely emotional and, as such, reactive and therefore unreliable. Our emotions move quickly and form impressions instantly. The ancient teachings of the Christian desert fathers and mothers used the term "passions" to describe intense feelings that can often spin out of control and obscure our vision. Cynthia Bourgeault, an author and teacher of the Wisdom tradition, clarifies the difference between the heart and the emotional center. "The heart, in the ancient sacred traditions, has a very specific and perhaps surprising meaning. It is not the seat of our personal affective life—or even, ultimately, of our personal identity—but an organ for the perception of divine purpose and beauty" (*The Wisdom Way of Knowing: Reclaiming an Ancient Tradition to Awaken the Heart*). What does it take to have a heart open enough for such perception to take hold?

The open heart

Several idioms describe hearts that are closed, broken, divided, or heavily laden with anger, regret, or resentment. The open heart may experience many of these, but it also has room enough for something more hospitable. A spacious heart is not an empty one, however. The latter entails a hollowness that we may try to fill with distractions or addictive behaviors. Spaciousness, on the other hand, is a hallowed experience that waits upon wisdom larger than our own. It brings a fruitfulness to the barren places within us and leaves us wide open to abundant grace.

Such spaciousness provides the turning point that characterizes true conversion. Without minimizing the importance of the mind and rational thought, religious language speaks strongly of a "change of heart" that draws us into an intimate relationship with God. This entwines the heart with the soul. The 16th-century mystic Teresa of Avila described this beautifully. In her book *The Interior Castle*, she used the analogy of a crystal castle as "inside our own souls, at the center of which the Beloved himself dwells." Within the castle are seven dwellings, each leading into the next and deepening the soul's immersion into prayer and union with the Beloved.

All of this may sound daunting and reserved for the holiest of the holy. In truth, spiritual life is available to all of us because we each have a heart. No matter how fast or slow it beats within the context of our daily lives, our heart provides both a place of grounding for our true needs and a guiding light for our innermost longings. Naming our heart's desire may be the best way to describe the listening that can lead us to a recognition of this Divine indwelling.

I found this to be so when I recognized the need to guard my heart in the midst of increasing hostility during the 2024 U.S. election season. As the tone of political rhetoric grew more profane and the culture wars gained steam, I feared the ugliness that might pervade my own heart. My husband, Ron, gave me John O'Donohue's book *Beauty: Rediscovering the True Sources of Compassion, Serenity, and Hope*, and I read it in slow and intentional fashion over the course of the year. Day by day, the concept of beauty unfolded and led me to recognize it as much more profound and pervasive than prettiness. Savoring O'Donohue's gorgeous prose and then journaling about it made me watchful for beauty in unlikely places. It also protected my heart from the kind of reactivity that is emotionally draining and mentally exhausting. The year's immersion into beauty provided an intentional way of viewing the world around and beyond me. As O'Donohue notes, "Seeing is not merely a physical act: the heart of vision is shaped by the state of soul. When the soul is alive to beauty, we begin to see life in a fresh and vital way."

My granddaughter's picture of valentine hearts on the first page of this chapter depicts the wondrous nature of the heart that is sometimes in perfect shape and at other times a bit off-kilter. The colors she chose remind me of the various shades that our inner hearts acquire through experiences of joy and sorrow, peace and anxiety, hope and despair, wonder and boredom. As we move further into an exploration of the heart's capacities, we might better appreciate the ancient proverb about vigilance that opens this chapter. Not only might we guard the heart against what might damage it; we can also gain a new appreciation for its life-giving potential.

PERSONAL REFLECTION

What is in your heart these days?

What protection does your heart need at this time in your life?

PERSONAL PRACTICE

Sketch in words or art the inner workings of your heart. How has it opened over the years? In what ways has it contracted? What concrete experiences, insights, and encounters have contributed to each of these responses?

GROUP CONVERSATION

What other idioms about the heart would you add to the list at the beginning of the chapter?

How would you describe the heart of your community, be it family, church, or neighborhood?

GROUP ACTION

Before your next gathering, take time to notice any heartfelt actions on your own part and in those around you. Be prepared to describe these to the rest of your group.

Heart Warmers

During the first years of our marriage, my husband, Ron, was stationed at a U.S. Coast Guard base in Sitka, Alaska. It was there that I met Father Jim Miller, a wise pastor with a kind and open heart. Soon after our arrival, I was elected president of the parish women's group. Along with offering their congratulations, the long-time members explained that I would now be in charge of the parish's annual bingo and raffle. Savvy to my newcomer status, they assured me that it would come together easily. As I started to make contacts, however, each woman began to withdraw. It became clear that the event had outlived its purpose and the group was tired of it. With most of the responsibility weighing on me, I turned to Father Miller for support. He guided me through it with generosity and good humor. In the end, he and Ron set up the parish hall without the help of the men's group, which had also retreated from sponsorship. Despite all of the disinterest, the event was an enormous success within the parish and the larger community.

Among the donated raffle items was an original painting by a local artist whose work was known throughout the country and therefore worth a small fortune. As the planning continued, I kept expressing my hope in winning it. When this went unrealized, I let it go. At the next group meeting, Father

Miller presented me with a few thank-you gifts. Among them was his own painting by the same artist. When I demurred, he assured me that it had given him joy and was now ready to be passed on. The painting's worth went way beyond its monetary value; it was an open-hearted gift of generosity and appreciation. It seemed only fitting that when Ron and I moved from Sitka, I passed it along to someone else.

Prayer

EXCERPT FROM "A MEDITATION AT THE FEAST OF SAINT VALENTINE," BY KEN PHILLIPS

O Power of Love,
Sustainer of All That Is,
Living Force of the Universe

I give thanks this day for those whose love has brought me into being...
for those whose love has shaped my journey...
and for those whose affection and care sustain me this day.

[Pause to name and remember those who have shaped your heart]

Through their generosity and love, my own heart has grown larger and more loving.
Amen.

2

"ICE AND ROCK" BY RON HENDRICKS

Hardness of Heart

"Gross is the heart of this people,
they will hardly hear with their ears,
they have closed their eyes..."

MATTHEW 13:15

These are hard-hearted times. Even so, they are not unique. Human capacity for cruelty and callousness, hatred and division, and verbal and physical violence is present throughout history. There is, however, a distinctiveness to our current moment. While there are limits to how much the internet and multimedia contribute to this malady, there is no question that our access to instant news, which is generally negative, and a siloed experience of social media have a significant impact. The Covid-19 pandemic and its resultant shutdowns and social isolation exacerbated the spread of misinformation that, in turn, gave rise to even more division. A pervasive sense of entitlement, along with perceived grievances, generate antipathy toward those with more control, power, and resources. Conversely, there is suspicion and resentment about those who are seen as freeloading off governmental assistance programs. All of this contributes to a hardness of heart in both individuals and communities.

John Mogabgab, the former editor of the spiritual journal *Weavings*, described the heart as the internal meeting point between a person and God. "The heart is the very core of our humanity, the place to which God turns in us and from which we turn, or refuse to turn, to God" ("Editor's Introduction," *Weavings*, Vol. X, no. 5). He employed the Greek term *sclerokardia* to describe the hardening of the heart in much the same way that the autoimmune disease scleroderma inflames and thickens the skin. *Sclerokardia*, he wrote, is a progressive disease in which "things that are not God slowly encase our innermost being in a rigid cocoon of stubborn, tragic alienation." Any number of distressing experiences might turn our hearts to stone: broken relationships, disappointments, failure, betrayal, simmering resentment, and empty promises. A number of idioms offer a glimpse into both the cause and the effect of such a state, such as heartsore, heartbroken, disheartened, and coldhearted, to name a few.

Anger's perils and possibilities

Fissures in our political, religious, educational, and cultural institutions are giving rise to increasing levels of anger and outrage. We see it everywhere. At the center of so many divisions is a perception that one is being dismissed, ignored, belittled, or disrespected. This, in turn, gives rise to tribalism, where those with the same grievances band together—often through social media—and nurse each other's outrage. Venting one's anger and frustration might bring some temporary relief, but it can also end up shredding relationships and giving one a worldview that is paranoid and perpetually unhappy. An opposite approach is equally unhelpful. Suppressing one's anger may lead to sarcasm and cynicism or to aggression and violence. It also has a polarizing effect that leads us far away from one another and from our own hearts.

In addition to its perils, anger holds possibility. It is difficult for someone with an open heart to ignore the pain and suffering caused by despots and systems of injustice and intolerance. To be "lion-hearted" is to engage with the world and seek ways toward peace, mutual understanding, and the rectifying of wrongs perpetrated in the name of one's nation, religion, or social order. "The wildness of anger's way, once harnessed, can be a formidable factor in the contest for justice and peace. The craving of anger's hunt, once tamed, can become hunger for the kingdom of righteousness" ("Editor's Introduction," John

Mogabgab, *Weavings*, Vol. IX, no. 2). Thus, to recognize one's anger but not allow it to go unchecked is a vital heartwarming practice. In being attentive to what enrages, offends, or infuriates us is a way of caring for our anger. In this way, we stop carrying what educator and author Parker Palmer describes as "false crosses"—those we place on ourselves by a deluded sense of what is happening around and to us. Pretending to be nice when we are filled with hurt and anger does not serve anyone well. Neither does brushing off someone else's violence toward us or others in a display of self-imposed martyrdom or fear of rocking the boat. Either way, we lose a valuable sense of connection with others.

A deficit of empathy

It could be said that indifference, rather than hate, is the opposite of love. In her book on the heart, Gail Godwin laments the pervasiveness of "heart absence" in herself and in the world around her. This may be the most chilling example of the hardened heart. As our lives grow increasingly isolated, our sense of empathy declines. Some see empathy not as a virtue but as a sign of weakness—or even, as one autocrat put it, the cause of civilization in decline. A well-known media figure caustically noted that turning the other cheek hasn't gotten us anywhere. Such attitudes, often pronounced by those professing to be Christian, reflect a deepening contempt for those seen as weak or a burden to society. It is a stunning and disheartening rejection of the beatitudes, which bless the meek, the poor in spirit, and the persecuted.

Some studies suggest that empathy surfaces early in our lives. As we mature, however, this capacity can dissipate. Excessive exposure to verbal and physical violence as well as information overload in the media numbs us, in time, to the realities of pain and human suffering. Cultural biases toward rugged individualism eschew any kind of meekness or dependency. Even those whose work and values center on helping others can suffer from compassion fatigue, a form of physical and emotional exhaustion that takes hold after prolonged exposure to the suffering of others. When it progresses, such fatigue can turn into cynicism and disdain for those they serve.

By recognizing that we are all in need of both human touch and Divine grace, we open our hearts to understanding, connection, and mutual respect.

In his First Letter to the Corinthians, Paul uses the analogy of the human body to describe the intricate connection between humans. When one hurts, all hurt; when one rejoices, we all rejoice. Empathy broadens our perspective, fosters mutual understanding, and underlies both compassion and kindness. By recognizing that we are all in need of both human touch and Divine grace, we open our hearts to understanding, connection, and mutual respect.

Losing touch with this intricate connection leads to increased polarization. This, in turn, fuels contempt for those whose ethnicity, race, religion, economic status, or political affiliation differs from our own. Not only do we fail to recognize the hurt or pain in someone else's life, but we may even find them unworthy of any concern or care. This is not new to our time, to be sure. People of color have known such contempt for centuries, even to the point of being classified as less than fully human or deserving of enslavement and persecution. The same holds true for people of various religions, sexual orientations, and physical or intellectual differences. Genocide can be justified by such attitudes because in denying others' humanity, it is easier to call for their eradication.

Thankfully, few of us go to such extremes. Even so, it is vital to recognize a tendency to scapegoat by blaming someone else for the disappointments, failures, or unfortunate circumstances in our lives. Franciscan friar and author Richard Rohr describes this tendency as hardwired into the human heart. "The sequence... goes something like this: we compare, we copy, we compete, we conflict, we conspire, we condemn, and we crucify. If we don't recognize some variation of this pattern within ourselves and put an end to it early on, it's almost inevitable" ("A Painful Pattern," Center for Action and Contemplation, March 24, 2024). Since we are all prone to such a tendency, we must be vigilant. Only by facing our own hard-heartedness can we chart a path toward softening it. Doing so takes attentiveness and attunement to what lies beneath the surface of our passions.

Holy longings

The Psalms contain some of the most heartfelt passages in the Bible. Of particular poignancy are those that express a deep longing.

> As the deer longs for streams of water,
>   so my soul longs for you, O God.
> My soul thirsts for God, the living God. PSALM 42:2–3

Notice the tender language used to describe a soul in search of comfort and consolation. It yearns and thirsts for God's compassionate and life-giving presence. These words describe the "holy longing" that theologian and author Ronald Rolheiser defines as the essence of spirituality. "There is within us...an unquenchable fire that renders us incapable, in this life, of ever coming to full peace" (*The Holy Longing*).

In my experience as a spiritual director, I often detect deeper longings underlying a directee's laments, regrets, questions, and quests. My primary role is listening beyond the words in order to draw attention to these yearnings. One need not be a spiritual counselor, however, to detect such longings in ourselves and others. If we pay attention, we can pierce the surface anger or frustration to better understand what generates such emotions. Often it is simply a desire to be heard and to be valued. This rings true for both our individual and communal desires.

Part of this longing is the search for God's consolation. Numerous "How long?" psalms plead for this presence. Many of them lament the agonizing silence and hiddenness of God that makes desperation all the more difficult.

> How long, Lord? Will you utterly forget me?
>   How long will you hide your face from me?
> How long must I carry sorrow in my soul,
>   grief in my heart day after day?
>
> PSALM 13:2–3

> How long, Lord? Will you hide forever?
>
> PSALM 89:47

There is sadness underlying the desperation in these pleas; it speaks of a soul that is "shuddering greatly" (Psalm 6:4). The root of the word "sad" means to be full or sated. Filling our lives with empty things—distractions, gadgets, busyness, meaningless relationships—only leads, in the end, to sadness. It also leads to unrest. Spirituality is what we then do with our unrest and leads us toward the pursuit of the Divine. "Once the soul awakens," John O'Donohue writes in *Anam Cara*, "the search begins and you can never go back. From then on, you are inflamed with a special longing that will never again let you linger in the lowlands of complacency and partial fulfillment." The desire for something more keeps us seeking the ultimate fulfillment that we only catch in glimpses. C.S. Lewis called these moments of "paradoxical joy"—ones that impel us to keep moving. Our hunger for the Divine presence intertwines with deeply human longings: to be understood, to be loved, to be heard, to be valued and respected, to be *home*.

Beyond our personal lamentations are those we feel for our country and our world. I mourn the loss of civility and of measuring our language so as to show a modicum of respect for others. As a writer, I find the overuse of a particular vulgar term in books, television programs, and film scripts not only offensive but also incredibly lazy. Words matter: the casual use of terms that demonize and demean leads to a decline in empathy and compassion.

Many of the psalms of lament were composed during times of exile. Such experiences cut people off from everything comforting, familiar, and secure. When the heart is in a state of exile, it separates from all that brings joy, peace, and a sense of belonging to something and Someone greater than ourselves.

The deep desire for belonging may lead us to assuage loneliness in online silos rather than actual community. It is here where contempt can grow as we identify more with the group than with a larger reality. In the process, we forget something vital—that we belong to each other.

This recognition makes the moaning of lament valuable and even hopeful. We may not have control over what happens to us or to the world around us, but we can choose how to respond. Lamentation may lead to a place of despair, but it can also break open the heart to greater understanding. Our aching joints might afford a bit more patience with those who move slowly or who have other physical ailments. Encountering the limits in our own lives allows greater latitude when we consider those whose options have been curtailed since birth. Facing the onslaught of lamentable news each day might impel us to darken our screens for longer periods of time to focus on something life-sustaining. As empathy increases, the vise around the heart loosens.

Defrosting the heart

Moving from a hard and closed heart to one that is tender and open is not an overnight process. Take another look at the photo of the stone at the beginning of this chapter. Its rough heart shape is reminiscent of the prophecy about the stony heart being replaced with one of flesh (Ezekiel 11:19). For me, the photo symbolizes a heart in process. The water around it initiates a thaw that works its way from the outer edges until the stone is liberated at last from its icy enclosure. In such a way, our own heart might find a warming process that draws out its humanity and restores the presence of empathy, kindness, understanding, and solidarity with others.

PERSONAL REFLECTION

What experiences, encounters, disappointments, or failures have hardened your heart?

As you prepare to read the next chapter, consider the ways in which your heart might grow warmer and more loving.

PERSONAL PRACTICE

Take an assessment of the factors that contribute to fear, resentment, anger, displacement, or entitlement in your life. In what way might you counter each one with something heartfelt and caring?

GROUP CONVERSATION

When and where do you encounter heart absence in your community?

When and where have you encountered warm-heartedness?

GROUP ACTION

Compose an accordion "How long?" psalm. Write the words "How long?" at the top of the page and invite someone to add a line to the psalm. Once they are finished, fold the paper over, accordion-style, so that line is hidden and pass the paper to the next person. When the psalm is complete, unfold the paper and read the words aloud. Reflect on the various longings expressed in the psalm.

Heart Warmers

When it came to politics, Dave and I were on opposite ends of the spectrum. He listened to conservative talk radio; I preferred NPR. He found a particular politician loathsome; I was ready to vote for her in a heartbeat. Even so, our working collaboration was warm and friendly. I was new to the publishing world and placed in a position that displayed my complete lack of expertise around sales projections and marketing plans. When facing a deadline that required exact numbers of print materials and promotional items, I was in a panic. Dave very calmly went through every line item and showed me how to calculate each one. It saved my job. When both of us were later let go, due to the company downsizing, he continued to be a supportive and caring presence for me.

So many of our polarizing issues pale in comparison to the more important ways we can connect and empathize with one another. Once we come to recognize the ability to help each other and to embrace our commonalities, we can set differences aside in a spirit of cooperation and caring. Dave passed away a few years ago. My memories of him are not of his political beliefs but rather of his kind and generous nature. That, in the end, is what endures.

Prayer

EXCERPT FROM "A MEDITATION AT THE FEAST OF SAINT VALENTINE," BY KEN PHILLIPS

Compassionate God,
I ask your help this day,
that I may be a more abundant reflection of Love;
that my words may be kinder to others,
  especially to those who tax my patience;
that my actions be more gracious to the human family,
  especially to those whose lives are especially in need
    of any signs of human attention.

[Pause and remember those in need]

May my thoughts be more care-full and compassionate,
  especially of those whom I tend to shut out
    or whom I make my enemy.
With hope in your compassion, I pray.
Amen.

3

"SACRED HEART" BY LINDA MCCRAY

A Heart of Flesh

And I will give them another heart and a new spirit I will put within them. From their bodies I will remove the hearts of stone, and give them hearts of flesh.

EZEKIEL 11:19

"When I see Papa, I just want to be close to him." This is how my four-year-old grandson, Clay, described his love for his grandfather. The two share a bond that began when we first provided childcare after his mother returned to work. From the beginning, the two grew close as Ron walked Clay back and forth prior to his nap and then read books, played games, and took him for wagon rides to a nearby playground.

This tender relationship illustrates how we gravitate toward those with warm hearts. These might be familial ties or ones generated through friendship, work, a religious community, or even chance encounters. I can name a number of people throughout my life whose warm hearts provided a place of sanctuary, safety, and serenity. There are also those whose art, music, poetry, or living witness moves our hearts toward something lovely and inspiring. And, of course, there are the "holy ones" whose vision and insight endures over time and offers a path toward a more loving and inclusive heart. One such experience began for me in an unconscious way long ago.

The Sacred Heart of Jesus

For over twenty years, I walked by a picture of the Sacred Heart of Jesus on the way to and from my bedroom each day. It hung alongside an image of the Immaculate Heart of Mary in our upstairs hallway. Because they were so familiar, I stopped paying attention to the pictures until I found the one of the Sacred Heart stashed among my parents' belongings after the death of my father. What stood out was the subtle outline of the heart and the warm glow that emanated from it. The gentle expression on the face of Jesus draws us toward the light that he promises and invites us to share.

Several years ago, I was asked to direct a women's retreat based on the theme of the Sacred Heart of Jesus and Immaculate Heart of Mary. Despite the hallway pictures and my Catholic upbringing, I was reticent about responding to the request. Neither of these devotions were part of my spirituality, and I was unsure about my ability to speak credibly about them. When I delved into the origins of each, however, I changed my mind.

The modern form of devotion to the Sacred Heart of Jesus begins with the story of a seventeenth-century French nun, St. Margaret Mary (Marguerite-Marie) Alacoque. She entered the convent at age twenty-four and had the first of a series of visions two years later. These lasted a year; she devoted the rest of her life to pondering their meaning and depth. Like many mystics, she resisted revealing the visions to others; she wanted the focus to remain completely on God and not on herself. In the last eighteen months of her life, a young priest who served as her spiritual director persuaded her to relate these visions in a series of letters. A year after her death, he published a book based on them: *The Devotion to the Sacred Heart of Our Lord Jesus Christ*.

In her visions, Margaret Mary saw "Christ's heart surrounded with rays brighter than the sun. Though transparent...the heart bore the wound given to him on the cross when the soldiers pierced his side with a spear" (Godwin). A crown of thorns surrounded the heart, and a cross appeared above it. Along with the image came the voice of Jesus telling her that he was no longer able to contain the flames of his love for humankind. He withdrew her own heart, placed it inside his own, and set it on fire. Then he replaced it inside her once again and named her a disciple of his most Sacred Heart. With this, he charged her with spreading the knowledge of his love to others.

One of the most striking aspects of this account is how it resembles the words of the prophet Ezekiel about replacing a stony heart with one made of flesh. In Margaret Mary's vision, what occurs is not simply a change but an *exchange* of hearts as Christ places hers within his own. Linda McCray's painting *Sacred Heart*, found at the beginning of this chapter, is a beautiful representation of the nestling of one heart within another. Light and warmth emanate from both. The larger heart of Christ appears porous, allowing beams of light to shine outward and illuminate the dark edges around it.

Conforming to the heart of Christ

In becoming familiar with the vision of Margaret Mary, I acquired a newfound regard for the imagery behind the Sacred Heart of Jesus. It not only deepens the connection with Ezekiel's "heart of flesh" but also illustrates what it means to conform our hearts to Christ. The great scientist, scholar, and theologian Pierre Teilhard de Chardin had a deep appreciation for the Sacred Heart of Jesus. His mother introduced him to the devotion when he was a child. Later in life, he wrote about its profound impact on him, particularly as he began to develop an understanding of the cosmic Christ. "There was no longer a patch of crimson in the centre of Jesus, but a glowing core of fire, whose splendor embraced every contour—first those of the God-Man—and then those of all things that lay within his ambience" (*The Heart of*

Matter). The heart as the center of our spiritual lives and as the Divine core from which love flows is key to recognizing Christ as the Alpha and Omega—the beginning and the end. It also deepens our understanding of true conversion and a turning of our hearts toward God.

The glowing heart in the hallway picture I passed each day growing up was a subtle and largely unconscious depiction of love, one that continues to unfold in meaning as I grow older. It reflects the light that glows within each of us and, when we don't obscure it with other concerns and distractions, shines brightly in us. This makes us part of the cosmic "ambience" enfolded into the expansive heart of Christ.

Another great mystic, Julian of Norwich, in *Revelations of Divine Love*, had her own way of viewing this pervasive presence of the Divine:

> See that I am in everything. See that I do everything. See that I have never stopped ordering my works, nor ever shall, eternally. See that I lead everything on to the conclusion I ordained for it before time began, by the same power, wisdom and love with which I made it.

Christian love is intrinsic. It is the lens through which we are able to view all of life as a free gift. This expands the concept of love beyond something we *do*; it is who we *are*, as made in the image and likeness of God. Richard Rohr describes the essential work of religion as helping us recognize this all-encompassing image of God in everyone and everything. "It is to mirror things correctly, deeply, and fully until all things know who they are. A mirror by its nature reflects impartially, equally, effortlessly, spontaneously, and endlessly. It does not produce the image,

nor does it filter the image according to its perceptions or preferences. *Authentic mirroring can only call forth what is already there*" (Center for Action and Contemplation Daily Meditation, "Mirroring the Mind of Christ," August 24, 2021).

For over four decades, I devoted myself to the ministry of catechesis. This included contributing to and speaking about catechetical resources and processes. I used to tell catechists that the most profound theological truth is taught to kindergarteners: "God loves you." Pure and simple. I have heard this described as "fluff" by those who think there should be more to the message than this. In truth, it may be one of the hardest beliefs to embrace. Little children grasp it easily. As we age, however, we begin qualifying it with caveats, such as: "God will love me *if*..." or "God loves me *when*...." This is a transactional notion of God's love: it essentially makes the free gift of love into something we can earn with good behavior and that is withdrawn when we misbehave. The vision of Christ expressing to Margaret Mary the overflowing love for humanity turns such a notion on its head. Being made in the image of God has nothing to do with our worthiness, our moral uprightness, or even our spiritual practices. All of those are helpful in opening ourselves to the mystery of Divine Love, freely given without measure or conditions and from which we can never be severed. We have assurance of this from one of the most eloquent passages in the New Testament: "For I am convinced that neither death, nor life, nor angels, nor principalities, nor present things, nor future things, nor powers, nor height, nor depth, nor any other creature will be able to separate us from the love of God in Christ Jesus our Lord" (Romans 8:38–39).

"For I am convinced that neither death, nor life, nor angels, nor principalities, nor present things, nor future things, nor powers, nor height, nor depth, nor any other creature will be able to separate us from the love of God in Christ Jesus our Lord"
(ROMANS 8:38–39).

Perhaps it is our own insecurity that can lead us to determine who God *doesn't* love. Author and activist Anne Lamott states it succinctly: "You can safely assume you've created God in your own image when it turns out that God hates all the same people you do." One of the signs of hard-heartedness is tribalism, in which our world shrinks to the point of excluding anyone who doesn't look, think, or believe like us. Paying attention to the triggers that lead us toward such entrenchment is a good starting point for softening our hearts. One effective path toward an open heart is listening to someone else's story. In doing so, we often find a connecting point that takes us beyond our biases and toward our commonality.

Moving to a heart of flesh

Two aspects of St. Margaret Mary's vision illustrate the movement toward a heart of flesh. One is the way her own heart was removed, placed within the heart of Jesus, and then reimplanted in her. There is such generosity in this gesture, as her heart is given a sacred place to abide. Psalm 23 is one of the most comforting passages in the Bible. It is often used at funerals and drawn upon during times of duress and suffering. The final verse offers a rich sentiment of hope in finding a place of welcome and respite: "Indeed, goodness and mercy will pursue me all the days of my life; I will dwell in the house of the Lord for endless days." Who among us does not want a safe and warm place to dwell? When offered such hospitality, we discover the joy of providing shelter for others and, in the process, become less fearful of who they might be and more accepting of who they are.

The second aspect was Margaret Mary's mission to spread knowledge of Christ's love to others. As noted earlier, this was an exchange in which her participation was central to the vision of love. Rather than leaving us holed up in a kind of spiritual hideaway, our own call toward an open and loving heart requires a response. In writing about the Sacred Heart of Jesus, Father James Martin invites meditation on some vital spiritual questions: "In what ways did Jesus love his disciples and friends? How did he love strangers and outcasts? How was he able to love his enemies? How did he show his love for humanity? What would it mean to love like Jesus did? What would it mean for me to have a heart like his? How can my heart become more 'sacred'?" (*America*, "Reviving the Sacred Heart," June 15, 2012). Martin goes on to emphasize how Jesus' love for us impels us to love others in imitation of Jesus. Doing so is what it means to have a "heart of flesh." It is one that contains some key attributes:

Fleshy hearts *feel*—they experience their own pain and empathize with the pain of others.

Fleshy hearts *expand*—they grow more loving through times of grief, loss, disappointment, and hurt as well as wonder, joy, peace, and love.

Fleshy hearts *care*—they attend to the woundedness in others with kindness, understanding, and patience.

Fleshy hearts *throb*—they are humble about their own frailties and recognize the need to seek and extend forgiveness and mercy.

Fleshy hearts *pulse*—they are grateful for and appreciate the everyday splendor of creation and all that it encompasses.

Fleshy hearts *beat* with regularity and strength—they remain consistent and measured despite the surface issues that may cause momentary flutters.

It is vital to monitor the heart to avoid overloading it with anxiety, misguided perfectionism, guilt, regret, shame, or compassion fatigue. The great visionary Hildegard of Bingen once wrote that there was nothing sadder than a drooping soul. As a medical practitioner, she advocated for the "greening power" of prayer and contemplation. Such a remedy keeps the internal glow warm and alive and the heart's rhythm intact. This in turn allows for a greater capacity for mercy.

The heart of mercy

"Blessed are the merciful, for they will be shown mercy" (Matthew 5:7). In multiple tributes to Pope Francis after his death, many people spoke directly or indirectly about his merciful heart. He regarded mercy as the primary message of Christ. This was apparent in the hospitality and generosity he showed to people from all walks of life and in his fierce advocacy for those living on the margins of society. What does it mean to be merciful, and why is it so central to a heart of flesh?

One misguided portrayal of mercy comes from classic melodramas. The villain corners the hero and, in a final act of triumph, insists that his nemesis beg for mercy. The audience is tempted to think for a moment that evil has defeated good as the hero is brought to his knees. It makes for interesting theater but poor theology.

Mercy stands predominantly in the hierarchy of virtues: Thomas Aquinas deemed it the greatest of them all, saying, "All the others revolve around it and, more than this, it makes up for their deficiencies." The virtues that spring from mercy are plentiful—forgiveness, compassion, kindness, understanding, respect, and, most of all, love. The beatitude states simply that those who extend mercy will receive it back from God, whose love would never drive us to our knees out of malice. Instead, we bow down in grateful recognition of the psalmist's words:

"The Lord is gracious and merciful, slow to anger and abounding in mercy" (Psalm 145:8).

The Hebrew word for mercy—*rechem*—is closely related to "womb." To abide in God's mercy is to be enfolded in womblike love. Scriptural pleas for a "clean heart" not only call for a release from guilt and torment but also express a deep longing for a more merciful life. It is one that engenders compassion and empathy, even in the most difficult circumstances. By making space for one another, we move into the world with a hospitable heart. It is one of the most effective means countering *sclerokardia* and opening ourselves to an exchange that places us within the Divine Heart of God's love.

PERSONAL REFLECTION

What experiences or encounters have softened your heart?

Name someone whose warm heart drew you close to them. What attributes contributed to that warmth?

PERSONAL PRACTICE

For the next day or two, keep a log of heartwarming actions or behaviors you encounter. Reflect on how each one affected you and how it warmed your own heart.

GROUP CONVERSATION

Revisit the list of attributes of a fleshy heart on page 34. What other ones could you name?

Revisit the questions posed by Father James Martin on pages 33 and 34. Which ones do you find most challenging and why?

GROUP ACTION

Decide on one or two concrete steps your group can take to generate ripples of mercy in your family, parish, neighborhood, or larger community.

Heart Warmers

I didn't meet my Aunt Ginny until I was eleven years old and she appeared at our home with her nineteen-year-old son. The visit was in preparation for their relocation to Denver—a stay that lasted only a year or two. I was immediately taken with her. She had beautiful black hair and soft brown eyes, much like my mother's. Mostly, I was drawn to her warm heart. One of my happiest memories is the celebration she planned for my twelfth birthday. It was a simple affair, held in her apartment and attended by my mother, cousin, and little brother. She made me feel special. For a girl on the verge of adolescence, it was a sacred experience of feeling cherished and appreciated.

It wasn't until several years after her death that I learned of her mental illness and her addictions to alcohol and prescription drugs. My mother mercifully withheld from me and my siblings the fact that Aunt Ginny died by suicide. Instead, we were told that she died peacefully in her sleep after an accidental drug overdose.

We sometimes draw close to warm hearts that are not always robust and healthy. Perhaps the vulnerability that comes through those that are damaged and wounded makes the glow from them all the more tender. All these years later, my Aunt Ginny is not defined in my mind by her illness or tragic death. What I cherish is her warm heart and my desire to draw close to it.

Prayer

Excerpt from "A Meditation at the Feast of Saint Valentine," by Ken Phillips

Merciful God,
I acknowledge this day
that I am connected to Loving Mystery
beyond my comprehension,
that my care for this planet is a necessary act
of mindfulness and appreciation,
and that I am nourished and enlivened by giving
and receiving affection.

[Pause and remember]

I also acknowledge that my love matters:
loving people is a good vocation;
attending to my emotional health and
physical well-being is appropriate and needed;
surrendering to love takes practice and time.

*[I pause and recall my various efforts to be loving
in my words and deeds]*

May I give my heart to you where it abides
within your mercy and grace.
Amen.

4

"OUR LADY OF SORROWS" BY WILLIAM HART MCNICHOLS

A Heart for Others

If one of your kindred is in need in any community in the land which the Lord, your God, is giving you, you shall not harden your heart nor close your hand against your kin who is in need.

DEUTERONOMY 15:7

Imagine receiving a birthday cake, complete with candles and singing, and then taking it to your room to eat all by yourself. It's like letting the air out of a balloon. Sharing is one of the great joys in life. The deepest experiences of sharing arise from the gift of generosity. As a counter to the restricted and self-guarded experience of stinginess, generosity opens the heart and blesses the soul. We not only find joy in giving but also appreciate in greater measure the abundance of God's gifts. Like the widow visited by the prophet Elijah whose jar of oil and bowl of flour never ran out, we discover the replenishing generosity of God. No wonder so many of the saints were joyous, even in suffering. They uncovered one of Jesus' most profound teachings: "Give and gifts will be given to you; a good measure, packed together, shaken down, and overflowing, will be poured into your lap. For the measure with which you measure will in return be measured out to you" (Luke 6:38).

The Heart Warmer stories I shared in the first three chapters illustrate ways in which the heart opens to others. In each case, I was the recipient of another's generosity. Father Miller gifted me with a valuable painting simply out of the desire to share the joy it gave to him. Dave provided not only professional assistance but also assurance that I was up to the job at hand. Aunt Ginny let me know I was loved and cherished. In addition to being filled with generosity, each heartwarming experience was suffused with caring. To care for another is to *attend* to them. Derived from the Latin *tendere*, which means "to hold," attending to others places our own needs and concerns in the background. The focus goes to the person within our circle of care.

As a Christian virtue, caring extends beyond our inner circles and into the broader world, particularly toward those who are most vulnerable. Jesus, the model caregiver, was so attentive to the needs of others that he could pick a feeble voice out of a crowd in order to heal a blind man (Mark 10:46–52). He was indiscriminate in his love, offering as much care to a beggar as to a Roman centurion. He also knew the importance of withdrawing from continual caregiving in order to replenish himself through prayer. And he didn't try to do it all himself but drew his disciples into the same kind of outreach. Through individual and communal acts of caring we, too, enter a great circle of love, one held within the expansive heart of God.

Sharing, generosity, and caring are virtues that we may jettison when entrapped by fear of the "other" or seduced by a mentality of entitlement. In hard-hearted times, we entrench and divide the world into those who are deserving and those who we think are not. Such attitudes are at the core of racist, xenophobic, misogynistic, and homophobic attitudes and actions that demonize those who don't fit into our version of who belongs and who doesn't. These are not the only times, of course, that initiatives against particular groups of people have been carried out. History is replete with accounts of genocide, pogroms, persecutions, and active campaigns against particular religious, ethnic, and cultural populations. Is it naïve to think that our own initiatives toward open-heartedness can change anything? If not, then what moves us toward open-heartedness, both as individuals and as a society? Once again, I turn for inspiration to an image that graced the hallway of my childhood home—the Immaculate Heart of Mary.

Mary's heart

This is not the Marian image that hung in our hallway, but it serves as a lovely companion to that of the Sacred Heart of Jesus image found in chapter 3. Both feature a subtle outline of the heart and a warm glow emanating from it.

Artistic depictions of the Immaculate Heart usually show Mary's heart pierced with a sword—a reference to the prophecy of Simeon during the visit to the temple by Mary, Joseph, and the infant Jesus:

> And Simeon blessed them and said to Mary his mother, "Behold, this child is destined for the fall and rise of many in Israel, and to be a sign that will be contradicted (and you yourself a sword will pierce) so that the thoughts of many hearts may be revealed."
>
> LUKE 2:34–35

The pierced heart is a formidable image for a young woman who was grounded in her love for God and devoted to the saving works of Jesus, even when she did not fully understand them (see Luke 2:41–50 and Matthew 12:47–50). While Simeon's prophecy was certainly troubling for Mary as a young mother, it becomes all the more heartbreaking when she stands at the foot of the cross many years later. The sharpest sword of all comes with the brutal execution of her son.

I was eighteen years old when I saw Michelangelo's *Pietà* on display at the Vatican. This was a few years before a disturbed man smashed parts of it with a hammer, necessitating its placement behind protective glass. At the time of my experience, the statue was situated behind a low railing inside St. Peter's Basilica, allowing a close-up view of the figures of Jesus and Mary. What stood out was the sorrow etched into Mary's face. I recalled it in vivid fashion several years later while holding my own child's lifeless body in my arms. My daughter's death at the age of one deepened my affinity with the sorrow that mothers bear in a particular way. The icon of *Our Lady of Sorrows* by Father William Hart McNichols, found at the beginning of this chapter, depicts this deep pain with tenderness and compassion. Mary's head, bent with the weight of sorrow, is supported by one hand, while the other seems to hold her broken heart. Heartbreak is evident in her sad eyes and downturned mouth.

Anyone acquainted with profound grief understands this portrayal. Is this what Simeon meant in the last part of his prophecy about "the thoughts of many hearts" being revealed? The sorrow in a personal experience can give rise to an empathic expansion of heart. As noted in chapter 2, there is an alarming decline in empathy in our world. This has led to an uptick in indifference toward minorities, immigrants, victims of war, and those living below the poverty line. Some of the actions taken toward them by those in positions of power have been vindictive and cruel. Worst of all is the justification of such actions as somehow "Christian." It makes the nurturing of empathy and compassion and the courage to stand for what is just all the more urgent.

The broken-open heart

Another striking aspect of Michelangelo's *Pietà* is the way Mary sits upright and supports Jesus' dead weight with grace and dignity. In order to portray this, the artist had to suspend strict attention to the figure's proportions. If Mary stood up, she would tower above most of us at nearly seven feet. This is no dainty maiden or fragile female who succumbs to the ravages of her grief. Instead, it is an image of a woman who, while well acquainted with sorrow, wasn't defeated by it. Her pierced heart opens her further to contemplation and compassion.

We see two instances of Mary's contemplative nature in Luke's gospel:

> After the visit from the shepherds, she reflects upon the wondrous events that have just taken place: "And Mary kept all these things, reflecting on them in her heart." LUKE 2:19

> When they find Jesus after he goes missing on the family's pilgrimage to Jerusalem, "He went down with them and came to Nazareth, and was obedient to them, and his mother kept all these things in her heart." LUKE 2:51

Mary is mostly a silent figure in the gospels, but in these accounts Luke conveys her observant nature. There were many puzzling, confusing, and fearsome experiences in her life as she watched Jesus grow and then move into his public ministry. While many legends grew around her over the centuries, what remains central is the quiet and contemplative figure in Luke's telling of the story. And the repository of her pondering is her broken-open heart.

In her book *My Grandfather's Blessings*, Rachel Naomi Remen tells about Glory, a young family doctor who attends a retreat for medical professionals dealing with the stress and heartache of tending to those who are sick and dying. During the first session, Glory shares how sadness has enveloped her since childhood. Despite this, she was sought out by those who were in deep physical and emotional pain. In a later session, Glory tells about a breakthrough she had while walking the labyrinth on the grounds of the retreat center. Recollecting the discovery of a pinecone that was split down the middle, she describes how it symbolized her own broken heart. "Suddenly she understood why others had come to her for refuge since her childhood. The suffering she was able to feel had made her trustworthy." Such a discovery brought her to the center of the labyrinth, where she knelt down "and for the first time since she was a child, she wept." Her broken-open heart was a place of refuge for those needing both physical healing and emotional warmth.

Contemporary culture often encourages us to escape our pain rather than reflect upon it. To that end, we have numerous ways to distract ourselves. To do so, however, is to bury something essential to an open heart. Mary's reflections and Glory's revelation offer an alternative to dismissing or denying our heartaches. Love, when it moves beyond sentimentality, becomes an avenue toward the vulnerability and heartbreak that besieged and transformed both women. This is what the priest and theologian Henri Nouwen described as a fall *into* love. "The Spirit of love says: 'Don't be afraid to let go of your need to control your own life. Let me fulfill the true desire of your heart'" (*Here and Now*).

Mary is also a model of a compassionate heart—open, vulnerable, and steadfast. She displays the kind of courage and fortitude one must have to surrender to the power of the Divine. To let go of control facilitates the movement into a deeper and more expansive heart space. We often don't do so willingly but rather through experiences of brokenness. When directing retreats on the theme of an open heart, I ask participants what breaks their hearts. Responses range from sadness due to an overall decline in compassion and empathy to personal experiences of loss, regret, disappointment, and severed relationships. Naming our heartaches is an important way to not only acknowledge them but also to embrace them.

In an online essay about the broken heart, Parker Palmer notes how violence occurs when we don't know what to do with our suffering. Such violence can be physical, but it is more often emotional and psychological. Consider those whose hearts have been shattered and who then take the shards and aim them at others. Palmer calls these "heart grenades"; they can explode with great fury or in subtle acts of sabotage. While this may be evident in interpersonal relationships, it also underlies the polarization that infects entire societies. When we listen for what lies below the contemptuous and noisy rhetoric, the hurt, pain, and fear become apparent.

Palmer calls for a different response to suffering, one that gives rise to a supple heart. It breaks open so as to increase the capacity for love, empathy, kindness, and compassion. "Instead of becoming bitter, resentful and withdrawn, [those with supple hearts] become more generous and engaged—not in spite of their pain but because of it. Suffering has opened their hearts and made them more understanding of others, more grateful for the gifts of life, even when things get tough" ("The Alchemy of the Broken Heart," Living the Questions with Parker J. Palmer, May 9, 2025).

There are some lovely synonyms for suppleness—elasticity, litheness, and limberness, to name a few. Athletes are well aware of the need to stretch their muscles and limber up their joints before engaging in vigorous activity. An expansion of the heart takes similar dedication. Being aware of the present moment, remaining attentive to our emotions, finding something for which to be grateful each day—all are intentional spiritual practices that keep the heart beating with warmth and caring. After my daughter's death, I found that sharing her story helped not only to ease my pain but also to connect me with others who knew something similar. Formal bereavement groups facilitate such a process, but everyday encounters can do the same. Sharing our stories keeps us from self-crafted martyrdom or an increasing sense of isolation and loneliness. I found this to be true when writing a book about my experience of grief and then sharing it with others. One story gives rise to another, and we begin to recognize the profound connection in Paul's description of the "one body." As Palmer writes, "What matters is that we remain faithful—faithful to our own gifts, faithful to the human needs that lie within our reach, and faithful to those moments when our gifts might help meet one of those needs."

Moving toward unity

The quest for unity runs deep within the human spirit, implanted there by a God of infinite union. The essence of Paul's image of One Body in Christ is incarnational reality—God's entry into the world in human form—and is much more widespread than we might imagine. When we embrace this, we come to see the Body of Christ as a living, breathing reality and not just a beautiful metaphor.

Like most realities, we first recognize it in our own human experience. Consider the disconnect many of us have with our own bodies. We sometimes pay more attention to the maintenance of our cars than we do our physical well-being. By setting aside healthy habits, we run ourselves into the ground. This will, in time, show itself in physical symptoms such as fatigue, illness, and a change in heart rate.

Even more damaging is the way we can be at war with ourselves. Thomas Merton wrote of the false self and its link to spiritual dis-ease. We work very hard at projecting images of ourselves in order to mask the parts we fear, repress, or feel ashamed of. Deep inadequacies have a way of showing up in one of two ways: through constant self-abasement or excessive self-aggrandizement. Each one emanates from a similar state of separation. Empathy increases when we allow ourselves to notice, feel, and embrace our own pain. This expands the capacity to relate to the pain of another while, at the same time, honoring how each person's pain is unique.

Transformation was at the heart of Jesus' teaching—that we would learn to see with new eyes and hear with new ears. It is a slow but steady movement toward oneness with Christ. We may not all move in complete sync with one another, but we are inching closer to the Omega point, as described by Teilhard de Chardin. This is the full realization of the energy of Christ's love "fusing all elements of creation [together] without losing their identity."

The hand of mercy

"Save me." "Heal me." "Make me whole." Over and over in the gospels, people beseech Jesus for his healing touch. And over and over again, he responds with the extended hand of mercy, forgiveness, and love. The only thing he asks of them is to trust. And to trust means letting go and yielding to the power of grace.

It is not an easy thing to do. In contemporary culture, yielding is not considered an important or even a desirable skill. When it comes to trusting in God's love and grace, however, we let go of the illusion of control to allow *possibility* to arise. This requires faith that goes beyond glib credos or impulsive actions. There has to be a level of consent to yield to such grace and to accept the extended hand of mercy. In *Showings*, Julian of Norwich described "beseeching"—a turning of the heart toward God and the most radical form of conversion—as "a true and life-giving lasting will of the soul which is owned and fastened to the will of our Lord, by the sweet and secret working of the Holy Spirit." Since this is not accomplished in a single leap of faith, how does one's heart reach such a turning point?

One of the most heartbreaking accounts in the gospels is that of Jesus praying through the night in the Garden of Gethsemane. It is there that he must yield, give over, trust, and let go. He exhibits the kind of humility that is the twin virtue to trust. This is why it is *by faith* that there is healing and restoration and the ability to walk on in the midst of suffering and loss, devastation and disappointment, betrayal and rejection. No matter what storms befall us, the hand of mercy reaches out to hold and heal, to assure and steady, to provide courage and strength. Then, through a humble recognition of our need for divine assistance, we are freed from the imprisonment of certainties and able to yield to the awesome dimension of possibility. This is the heart of hope: out of darkness comes light; out of death comes life; out of letting go comes the extension of grace. The extended hand also reminds us that we are not alone and that we can offer the same mercy to others.

Breathing with and for others

Singing with a women's choir is one way I found to keep my heart open during a time of cultural and political division. In addition to the joy of singing and learning new and challenging music, I gleaned numerous lessons applicable to the heart. One of those occurred during a rehearsal for our annual Christmas concert. At one point, our director stopped our flailing attempts to hold a sustained note. She went on to demonstrate what happens when you struggle to pump out the last bit of air in your now-depleted lungs. The note sours and goes flat and your face contorts into one of agony and desperation. Not a great look for a choir singing about the joys of Yuletide! She encouraged us to breathe before reaching this point and reminded us that the rest of the group would sustain the note in our brief absence. In other words, we could rest assured that others would breathe for and with us.

This serves as an apt metaphor for the times when our spiritual capacities are worn down by overload, exhaustion, perfectionism, or any other obstacle to a healthy and happy heart. During such times, it is important to remember that ours is not the only voice in the choir. I can think of a number of sustained notes in our lives—those times when we keep trying to sing despite the depletion of our inner resources. Grief is one. So, too, is an inflated sense of our own importance. Sad to say, some of the most breathless people I have come across are those involved in serving others: ministers, medical professionals, caregivers, teachers, parents. Their generous nature can lead them to take on more responsibility than their hearts—and lungs—can bear. Knowing we are part of a large choir of diverse, talented, and caring people liberates us from going solo and instead leaves the singing to others while we take a much-needed breath of fresh, restorative air.

We might also use our lung capacity to sustain others. Buddhists have a spiritual practice called *tonglen* in which an exchange of breath both acknowledges and releases the pain in our own hearts and in those of others. Pema Chödrön, a Tibetan Buddhist nun, describes how this works in her book *When Things Fall Apart*: "Whenever we encounter suffering in any form, the tonglen instruction is to breathe it in with the wish that everyone could be free of pain. Whenever we encounter happiness in any form, the instruction is to breathe it out, send it out, with the wish that everyone could feel joy." This helps to dissolve the walls we build around our hearts. There is a beautiful connection in this practice with that of the Sacred Heart of Jesus, in which our own hearts are given shelter. Nourished with grace and nestled within this larger, expansive heart of cosmic love, we experience the glowing "core of fire" that Teilhard de Chardin describes as the consummation of Christ's love.

Moving beyond the heartache

My mother died on the feast of Our Lady of Sorrows (September 15). Because she was often so upbeat and given to easy laughter, it seemed incongruous. Even so, I recall how she turned to Mary in intercessory prayer when weighed down by weariness or anxiety. As I came to fuller knowledge of the heartaches she bore, the connection with Mary's sorrowful heart acquired more meaning.

In his book *Cherished Belonging*, Father Gregory Boyle tells about the trauma and despair that draw young people into lives of self-destruction and violence, particularly through membership in gangs. Once they start to recognize the wounds they carry through the love and acceptance of a nurturing community, they are able to embrace their inherent self-worth. Rather than obliterate the memory of the trauma, they let go of their attachment to it. This may explain why those with broken-open hearts can be so warm and caring. It rang true with my mother. Her sorrows didn't define her but instead gave way to an expansive and hospitable heart.

No matter how deep our own experiences of heartbreak, we can learn from the way Mary held her sorrows and reflected on them. In doing so, we carry forward the ancient prophecy as we allow our own "thoughts of the heart" to emerge and lead us toward an interior space of contemplation and openness.

PERSONAL REFLECTION

Take some time to reflect upon the icon of Our Lady of Sorrows at the beginning of this chapter. What does this image evoke in you? What sorrow leaves you bent over with pain and sadness?

How have the wounds in your own life given rise to empathy and compassion for the pain of others?

PERSONAL PRACTICE

Intercession is a practice of praying on behalf of others. So often these prayers are centered on outcomes. The *tonglen* practice described in this chapter is an example of simply holding another's broken heart within our own. Consider someone you know or know about who is suffering. Breathe in their heartache. Breathe out consolation and peace. Let this prayer move through you.

GROUP CONVERSATION

What is the difference between a broken heart and a broken-open heart?

What might give rise to a heart that is transformed and enlarged by suffering?

ACTION

Before the next gathering, make an intentional effort to listen to someone who has a different point of view or who is struggling to handle something difficult in their life. When your group reconvenes, share how this effort brought a deeper understanding of something underlying these views and issues.

Heart Warmers

Virgie stopped by my classroom each afternoon before beginning her task of cleaning the school. After sharing a bit of news about current events on the nearby reserve where she lived, she would express how blessed she was. Knowing of the many tragedies she experienced—the violent deaths of three of her four sons and life with a chronic and sometimes violent alcoholic husband—made me wonder how she could hold such an expansive view of her life.

I was 23 at the time and serving a three-year commitment as a volunteer teacher at a Catholic school in northern British Columbia. The mostly Indigenous population of the town and the student body was a far cry from my middle-class upbringing in Colorado. Virgie's heartbreaking experiences were ones that many others in her community also faced. Rather than making her heart brittle and resentful, however, each one seemed to make her more generous and grateful. She regularly gifted the volunteers with bannock—a delicious pan-fried bread—and embroidered moosehide moccasins with lovely beaded designs. I still have the pair she made for my infant daughter. As an Elder in her Band, she, with her kind heart, gave counsel and guidance up until the time of her death. Virgie's broken-open heart provided healing and refuge for so many in her community. She exemplified what it means to be empathetic, compassionate, and caring.

Prayer

EXCERPT FROM "A MEDITATION AT THE FEAST OF SAINT VALENTINE," BY KEN PHILLIPS

I open my heart to you, O God.

Make me mindful this day of the signs of Love
that are all around me:
of good words spoken,
of gentle touch extended,
of important things that spring from appreciation
and true passion,
of deeds that are born of generosity
and of real understanding.

[Pause and open my heart to being loved]

Mend my brokenness and make me more loving,
expansive,
and ever aware of your continual presence.
Amen.

5

"BEAUTY UNFOLDING" BY RON HENDRICKS

The Contemplative Heart

"Blessed are the clean of heart, for they will see God."

MATTHEW 5:8

Heartwood is the inner part of a redwood tree's trunk. While composed of dead cells, it provides vital structural and life-giving support to the tree and protects it from dangerous pathogens. Its dark reddish-brown color comes from the presence of tannins, which also serve to resist decay. The heartwood acts as a core for these magnificent trees and contributes to their durability.

It also provides a useful metaphor for the core that generates openness and growth of the human heart. Indeed, the word "core" has its origins in the Old French and Latin *cor* or *coeur*, meaning "heart." This interior space is one of the beatitudes listed in the Gospel of Matthew. Various translations name the heart as "clean" or "pure." My favorite is "single-hearted." It denotes the kind of internal hub that makes the outer aspects of our lives strong and sturdy, able to withstand the pathogens of division and antipathy toward others.

The word "courage" also has its roots in the heart and has a strong connection with this internal strength. We often associate courage with bravery, but there is a key difference between them. One is largely internal, while the other is external. The French root for brave is *braverie*, meaning to be brave or to face boldly. "While *bravery* denotes the idea of reckless, combative action, *courage* means acting from a faithful, trusting heart. The expression *having the courage of one's convictions* preserves something of this meaning" ("Courage as the Heart of Faith", W. Paul Jones, *Weavings*, Vol. XII, no. 3). Those with courage are not given to rash acts of bravado but have the measured strength of will that comes from within. The stability of our internal heartwood keeps us from becoming faint or falsehearted.

From reaction to response

In addition to their impressive stature, redwoods have an amazing lifespan. Some live for more than 2,000 years! Their size and stability enable them to withstand natural elements that would topple a smaller tree. They actually regenerate through fire.

In a similar fashion, it is often the fire-tested experiences in our own lives that teach us how to remain stable in the midst of external chaos. This moves us from reactivity to response; from being caught up in the drama of the moment to recognizing a larger and more hopeful reality; from a primitive reflex action to receptivity. In short, to a contemplative heart.

The words "contemplation" and "contemplative" might throw us off if we regard them as reserved for those in monastic life. When coupled with practices of responsiveness, awareness, and receptivity, however, the concept is much more accessible. It also becomes essential for a softening of the heart. Like the heartwood within the redwood tree, the heart remains stalwart and strong, despite the winds that might buffet it. "Within the contemplative heart you are indestructible, even though you feel quite vulnerable and unsure of yourself in many ways," says Cynthia Bourgeault ("The Way of the Heart," *Parabola*, January 31, 2017). Such a heart is especially vital during times of upheaval and division.

In 2024, I was invited by Boston College's Clough School of Theology and Ministry to write a course for their online Crossroads program. Entitled "Faithful Unity Amid Polarization," its focus was on facing the divisive issues in the Church and society with a more compassionate response. A key resource for the course was a video presentation by Brian D. Robinette, associate professor of theology at Boston College. After defining some of the reasons for the deep polarization in our religious and political spheres, he delved into the responsiveness that comes from a contemplative outlook. It calls for the kind of "inner room" stance that Jesus names. "But when you pray, go to your inner room, close the door, and pray to your Father in secret. And your Father who sees in secret will repay you" (Matthew 6:6).

This call to an inner room is more a state of the heart than a physical space. With so many ways for the outer world to encroach upon the interior one, finding this space can be challenging. What, then, does a contemplative heart entail? In order to surface an answer, it helps to clarify the meaning of contemplation. It can be described in various ways: resting in God, enlarging our vision, tamping down internal turmoil, being in the moment. Implied in each is a settling of sorts, one that allows the outer stimuli to be tuned out while we find a core of serenity within ourselves. There is also a strong connection with seeing in a clearer way. Thomas Merton described contemplation as moving from opaqueness to transparency. Evagrius Ponticus, one of the desert fathers, called it a vision of the nature of things (*physika*) and likened it to removing, one by one, the blindfolds that obstruct such clear sight. In *Dance of the Spirit*, educator and author Maria Harris called it "gazing at something with an uncluttered view." It is an awakening to and mindfulness of being "in the presence of more than ourselves—...a form of prayer."

Contemplation not only lifts the veil from our own vision but also provides a more compassionate and empathetic gaze toward others. The Latin for person—*personare*—means "sounding through." A contemplative life is one in which we sound through to one another, opening ourselves to a vulnerability that allows others to see the beauty, truth, and love in us and allows us to recognize the same in them. Unless we are living the life of a recluse, each of us is bound to struggle with people we don't like, trust, or care to be around. Rather than writing them off with a contemptuous or dismissive characterization, contemplation invites us to consider them as persons. This does not mean becoming targets for other's neuroses, abuse, or bad behavior. Instead, we seek to love in a way that opens our vision to those we might otherwise remain blind to.

Listening with heart

One of the most important ways to "sound through" is by being present to and with someone else. Listening with an open heart is part of this practice. It is key to spiritual companionship as well as to basic respect for the other. One of the biggest causes of upset in my grandchildren is when they think I am not listening to them. Underlying this complaint is a feeling of being dismissed or ignored. This is true for adults as well. We often see this in the aftermath of a political party's loss. Pollsters and pundits name a failure to listen to the needs, ideas, and opinions of constituents as a primary reason for the defeat. It also explains why platitudes are so distasteful; they show an inattentiveness to and dismissal of another person's worth.

Listening with an open heart is a deeply contemplative practice. It removes us from self-centeredness to honoring and respecting another person. In listening deeply to another, we become attuned to our shared humanity and to the unique beauty we each possess. Such a practice breaks down barriers and connects us at a heart-to-heart level.

With so many ways to be distracted, being present to others as well as to ourselves can be a challenge. When we approach it with a contemplative heart, however, we discover the richness that each moment holds. It restores stability to our inner core and brings a lovely grounding of peace. "When I am present—to prayer, to art, to another—the feeling I have, incommunicable as it may be, comes to me as a deep tone, the note of a cello rather than of a violin," writes Mary Rose O'Reilley ("Deep Listening: An Experimental Friendship," *Weavings*, Vol. IX, no. 3). There is a softening that takes place when we allow that deep note to resonate within us. It draws us into the Divine heart through a contemplative way of prayer.

Prayer of the heart

In my years as a catechetical consultant, I offered presentations and retreats on the topic of prayer to groups of catechists, parish and diocesan leaders, Catholic school teachers, parents, and many others. As part of these sessions, I often heard the same lament: "I know how to say prayers, but I am not sure I know how to pray." There is an important difference. Because so many of us were taught to memorize prayers as children, this is the form we are most accustomed to. There is beauty in this way of praying, to be sure, but it offers just one way of praying that opens the heart.

There is no shortage of books and other resources that serve as useful guides into various forms and expressions of prayer. When linked with the contemplative heart, prayer simply arises from our deepest yearnings, hopes, desires, and love. During my presentations on prayer, I often ask the group this question: *Where do you experience closeness with God?* It doesn't take long for responses to pour forth—in nature, with my children or grandchildren, listening to music, being in church with a cherished community. What these responses hold in common is immersion into the present moment.

In addition to spending a year in search of beauty, I adopted two practices as a way to guard my heart from the toxic environment of fear and division during the U.S. election campaign. As noted earlier, one was singing with the women's choral group, the Noteables. Attending weekly rehearsals entailed two hours doing nothing more than singing and learning how to increase my vocal capacity. I often left with fresh insights into the beauty of singing with others and lessons learned from modulation and attentiveness, such as the breathing technique that reminded me of the connection and support we provide to each other.

The second practice was baking sourdough bread. After a bumpy beginning, when I thought I had killed the starter, I began to get the hang of preferment, bowl folds, and proofing times. The whole process of mixing and measuring, kneading and shaping, resting and baking is very tactile. It catches me up in the moment and provides a lovely rhythm that results in a satisfying and delicious outcome.

I rarely offer a presentation on spirituality or direct a retreat without mentioning gratefulness as an essential practice. As such, it settles into the heart and forms an outlook on life that sees all as blessing from a God of never-ending abundance. As Thomas Merton wrote, "To be grateful is to recognize the Love of God in everything [God] has given us—and [God] has given us everything" (*Thoughts in Solitude*, 33). Gratitude transforms our vision, allowing us to see these great gifts with open minds and clear eyes. What response can we make other than to give thanks and praise to God from whom all blessings flow? While it is easy to be grateful during times of ease and plenty, it takes a

When we see life as a *gift* and not a *given*, we are more likely to share all that we cherish and enjoy with others.

wider vision to do so during experiences of suffering, disappointment, disillusionment, and loss. This is why it takes discipline to fold gratitude into our daily lives. In order to do so, it requires a "contemplative outlook" in which we stop on a regular basis to reflect on everyday grace. This, in turn, gives rise to generosity. When we see life as a *gift* and not a *given*, we are more likely to share all that we cherish and enjoy with others.

In his book *Music of Silence*, Brother David Steindl-Rast offers a lovely explanation and application of the eight movements of the Liturgy of the Hours. Writing about the evening prayer of Vespers, he notes how humans have a desire for a place of serenity where we can piece together the disparate parts of our days. He writes that "prayer is not sending an order and expecting it to be fulfilled. Prayer is attuning yourself to the life of the world, to love, the force that moves the sun and the moon and the stars." While there are structured ways to do this, attuning ourselves to the present might happen through harmonizing with others or kneading a mound of dough. Either way, it becomes a mystical experience.

A mystical view

"Mysticism" is another term that we might associate with those living in blissful solitude. Richard Rohr notes how "the word itself has become relegated to a 'misty' and distant realm that implies it is only available to very few and something not to be trusted, much less attractive or desirable" ("Disciples, Prophets, and Mystics," Center for Action and Contemplation, March 18, 2020). He goes on to define the mystic as one with experiential knowledge. I would describe it as a way of knowing from the heart. Many mystics, such as Teresa of Avila, Catherine of Siena, and Julian of Norwich, were known for their visions of the Divine. Some of their accounts might make us blush, as if we are peeking into something way too intimate for a third person's eyes to behold. This is what embodies a visionary, however. Their profoundly intimate encounter with God is ultimately transformative. It makes it hard to distinguish life apart from God. Mechtild of Magdeburg described this beautifully: "The day of my spiritual awakening was the day I saw and knew I saw all things in God and God in all things." This marks a profound difference from the self-centeredness that characterizes a hardened heart. The narcissist says, "Look at me"; the mystic says, "Look at God." Mechtild's vision doesn't preclude her life but instead sees it glimmering with God's loveliness and mercy.

In chapter 1, I noted how I spent a year focused on beauty. Guided each day with a slow reading of John O'Donohue's book *Beauty: Rediscovering the True Sources of Compassion, Serenity, and Hope*, I embarked on a daily quest for beauty. In the book's introduction, O'Donohue notes how contemporary crises can be traced to our inattentiveness to beauty. Without it, we enlarge a tolerance for coarseness, ugliness, and cruelty. What better ways to harden the heart? By contrast, "when we expect and engage the Beautiful, a new fluency is set free within us and between us. The heart becomes rekindled and our lives brighten with unexpected courage." This in turn gives rise to hope. "Courage is amazing because it can tap in to the heart of fear, taking that frightened energy and turning it towards initiative, creativity, action, and hope." Such fluency changes the picture. When viewed through a contemplative lens, we acquire a capacity for seeing the world as transparent rather than opaque.

Reverence is way toward this vision and a powerful counter to the distressing rise in profanity in our culture. By viewing the world as transparent, we notice things that might easily bypass our vision. Nature provides numerous ways to enlarge our visual senses. It also offers a valuable perspective that places us within a larger context. "Reverence may take all kinds of forms, depending on what it is that awakens awe in you by reminding you of your true size," says Barbara Brown Taylor in *An Altar in the World*. "Nature is full of things bigger and more powerful than human beings, including but not limited to night skies, oceans, thunderstorms, deserts, grizzly bears, earthquakes, and rain-swollen rivers." Reverence regards all ground as holy and each moment an opportunity to open our eyes to a world of wonder beyond our wildest imagination.

Self-knowledge

The mystical vision isn't something out of this world; rather, it is grounded *in* this world by recognizing what lies beneath current issues and tensions. This takes some spiritual discipline and a willingness to let go of certain behaviors and attitudes. Lovely as it would be to have a step-by-step solution to the problems that beset our individual and collective mindsets, we must recognize the challenges that come with a contemplative heart. This includes an honest acceptance of who we are.

One of the things I find most intriguing about mystics like Teresa of Avila and Julian of Norwich is the importance they placed on self-knowledge. Humility is a central virtue in this process. Although sometimes mistakenly understood as self-abasement, it is, in fact, the ability to see ourselves for who we are. As a virtue, placing God as the source of all that is good, we keep our egos in check by neither inflating nor deflating ourselves. Derived from the Latin word *humus*, meaning earth or clay, humility is a recognition not of our lowliness but of our grounding in God's creative love. The word "human" comes from the same root. Thus, to "walk humbly with" our God, as the prophet Micah (6:8) wrote, is to recognize our worth in the eyes of God. It also helps us to value all of God's creation. Such a perspective gives rise to humble praise for who we are and for what God, in infinite goodness, has given to us.

One of the most tragic aspects of an opaque vision is the inability to recognize the beauty in ourselves. "No-one was sent into the world without being given the infinite possibilities of the heart. It is sad that so many of us go through our lives without ever seeming to discover the depth and beauty of the heart," writes John O'Donohue in *Beauty*. A key element of this discovery comes from not trying to mask, deny, or bury our feelings—something I touched upon in chapter 4. As a child, I absorbed a message about the importance of "being nice." It led to lots of needless shame over feeling angry or frustrated and trying to fake my way through unpleasant encounters. To be sure, there is a need for reining in one's worst instincts. It becomes harmful, however, when it gives rise to passive-aggressive behavior or pent-up emotions that explode in fury once they can no longer be contained. Feelings of hurt, pain, suffering, disappointment, anger, grief, and sadness are part of life. They also have much to teach us if we are attentive to what underlies them. Those who do find a way to transform their pain into something generous and life-giving. In O'Donohue's words, "In silence and solitude, the contemplative has learned the mysteries of the heart's fragility, smallness and darkness." This enables a breaking through to one's "inner sanctuary." The heart of my friend Virgie exemplified this. The numerous tragedies in her life seemed to make her more generous and compassionate (see Heart Warmers, chapter 3).

An expansion of compassion

In the video presentation for the Boston College course on polarization, Brian Robinette notes how contemplation offers a path beyond polarization by enlarging our capacity for compassion. Contemplative awareness, he says, offers "a spacious quality that allows our feelings and thoughts to be present without reacting to them. This being present is, in fact, a basic kindness, a simple warmth that allows feeling and thought patterns to unwind and express a deeper wisdom and compassion" ("Christian Contemplative Practice in Polarized Times," https://www.youtube.com/watch?v=Ja_NHgdnfNE).

In writing a book about grief over the long term, I explored how deep loss has the potential to open the heart to others through the sharing of stories and experiences. I knew this in a very personal way after my daughter's death and amid other painful losses. Such an experience makes the promise of the "coming of the kingdom" recognizable in the here and now. It is all too easy to miss, however, when we are caught up with daily responsibilities and endless distractions. Experiences of exquisite joy and beauty awaken us to this reality. Living in a Colorado mountain town, I receive daily glimpses of nature's wonders each time I look out the front door. Paradoxically, times of deep sorrow also hold the potential for attuning us to the presence of this divine space. In his book *Learning to Pray*, Wayne Muller offers a beautiful insight into the line "thy kingdom come." "The first thing we see—the experience that invariably presents itself with the most dramatic flourish—is the unbearable, the unspeakable, the sorrow deeper than words... But curiously, when we remain still and awake in the country of sorrow, we invoke a gradual willingness to imagine a simultaneous emergence of grace, of some hidden wholeness. Sam Lewis, the beloved Sufi master, would often say, 'It is not a matter of when you reach the kingdom of heaven. It is a matter of when the kingdom of heaven reaches you.'"

One common thread weaving through the lives and visions of mystics is that of suffering as a gateway into empathy and unity with others. As noted earlier, Teresa of Avila's book *The Interior Castle* describes the ever-deepening spiritual journey through seven chambers of the soul. Rather than leading us to a space of internal insulation from the suffering of the world, such a path draws us more deeply into it. A broken-open heart is naturally one of empathy and contains a desire to, in Teresa's words, "help the crucified in some manifest way."

An understanding of sacramentality—that of God being present to us in the midst of our everyday interactions, symbols, rituals, and relationships—holds great promise for a unity of heart and sacred regard for the common good. In the end, it comes down to kinship: a radical knowledge that we not only belong together but that we *belong to* each other. With a deeply contemplative vision, we then recognize the circle of compassion that will heal our divisions and enable us to recognize ourselves mirrored in one another. "The two longings deepest in your heart—the longing to love and to be loved—are the stirring of God within you. Your capacity to care is God. It is your beauty," says O'Donohue. This forms a rhythm of life, of caring for others as we carry out daily routines. God is not waiting in some faraway place but accompanies us as we exit the center of stillness. In so doing, we are able to engage with the activity that is part of being a living thing. When we come to a recognition of this, everything changes.

A heart within a Heart

> It is a great understanding to see and know inwardly
> that God, who is our Creator, dwells in our soul,
> and it is a far greater understanding to see and know
> inwardly that our soul, which is created, dwells in God.
>
> JULIAN OF NORWICH, *SHOWINGS*

Julian's vision resembles that of St. Margaret Mary and the encasement of her heart within the Sacred Heart of Christ. Both women recognize the indwelling of the Divine within themselves. What draws them further is the indwelling of themselves in God. Teilhard de Chardin called this the "divine milieu." "In the divine milieu, all the elements of the universe touch each other by that which is most inward and ultimate in them. There they concentrate, little by little, all that is purest and most attractive in them without loss and without danger of subsequent corruption," he writes in *The Divine Milieu*. The psalmist describes this desire in poetic fashion: "One thing I ask of the Lord; this I seek: To dwell in the Lord's house all the days of my life, To gaze on the Lord's beauty, to visit his temple" (Psalm 27:4).

Much like Teresa's interior castle, the dwelling place is a state of heart and soul. If it is true that we all dwell in God, then there is no reason to see ourselves as apart from one another. Not only do we feel each other's joys and pains, but we also share a space in which we can embrace all as part of ourselves. No more "othering," since we are swimming in the same mystical sea. Like the photo of the rose at the beginning of this chapter, we see beauty unfolding in ever-increasing ways as we begin to see as Christ sees and love as Christ loves. "God is the atmosphere where our essence clarifies, where all falsity and pretention vanish," O'Donohue writes. "Here we are utterly enfolded." Just as the rose expands outward, so do we. Our personal concerns give way to those that embrace the common good; we want the beauty of Divine love to reach others as much as we want it to reach us.

A different way of peace

My two grandchildren offered an example of this while discussing what it would be like to have magical powers. At first, their imaginations centered on the pleasant experiences they could conjure up at will. Then they began to include others. Four-year-old Clay described how they could use their magic to show others how to be kind and caring. It was such a sweet and innocent view of life as well as a basic recognition of the importance of a warm and open heart.

There is nothing magical about contemplation, however. It isn't a solution to anything but a *response* to hardened times and a gentle way of living in the midst of them. Contemplation also doesn't imply a serene existence. The heart will still be troubled—perhaps more so—because of its increased vulnerability and tenderness. The wounds we carry have the potential to deepen our faith, expand our hope, and increase our love. What is required is remaining open to them. In doing so, we experience a peace that is outside of this world.

As mentioned earlier, Father Gregory Boyle has seen more than his fair share of wounded people. His ministry through Homeboy Industries brings him in touch with those whose lives have been pierced by abuse, violence, and hardship. Yet, he bears witness to the kind of healing that comes from those who carry their wounds with courage and hope. In *Cherished Belonging*, he describes the peace that Jesus brings to disciples huddled in fear: "It's not for nuthin' that the one who enters the locked room after the Crucifixion and says, 'Peace,' was the one bearing wounds. He carries them. He doesn't move beyond them; he moves with them in the room. Not merely tolerating but, indeed, embracing them. He makes friends with the wounds. We don't move on from trauma but learn to move with it."

The heart knowledge that provides steadiness, courage, and peace comes from being nestled within something larger than ourselves. The very heart of God provides shelter large enough to hold us all.

The heart knowledge that provides steadiness, courage, and peace comes from being nestled within something larger than ourselves. The very heart of God provides shelter large enough to hold us all. Nothing is asked of us but to remain open and receptive. There are no worthiness tests, no secret passwords, no room for the baggage of guilt or shame we carry. "This is the subversive consolation of God, the sweet mercy that sees beyond our blunders and failures... God is the atmosphere where our essence clarifies, where all falsity and pretension vanish. Here we are utterly enfolded," O'Donohue tells us.

An unshakable steadiness comes from knowing that we are nestled securely within a larger heart of Love. Within it we can walk with gratitude, reverence, humility, and the peace that comes from an openness of heart and generosity of spirit.

The heart's desire

> I did not have to ask my heart what it wanted
> because of all the desires
>   I have ever known,
> just one did I cling to
> for it was the essence of all desire:
>   to know beauty.
>
> ST. JOHN OF THE CROSS

At the beginning of the book, I referred to the discovery about beauty that led me to see it as something much larger than prettiness. The increasingly divisive tone of the nation's politics was an impetus behind the quest but, as the year unfolded, I began to recognize a deeper and more heartfelt desire. To "know beauty" is to delve within ourselves and to come to the recognition of something we hold in common: the longing to love and to be loved. O'Donohue notes how these are not simply psychological or emotional needs but are the stirring of God within us. "Your capacity to care is God: it is your beauty."

Becoming a grandmother was a life-changing experience for me. It has expanded my heart in ways I never expected. Perhaps it is because there is a spaciousness in the love I have for my grandchildren that is unlike anything I have known before. It also brings a deep desire to be for them a graceful presence. I know my time with them will be limited, and so it is vital that I use it well and in the most beautiful way possible: to love them and to take in their love with gratitude and joy.

Is this the kind of love God holds for us? I believe so. We make it much more complicated when we tangle it up with expectations around which words or groups or behaviors or attitudes are required to earn such love. *God loves you.* This simple lesson, taught to kindergarteners, is truly the best news we could embrace. To love God is to love what God loves—which is everything *as it is*—and to strive to share that love with others. To open our hearts to all that is and to follow its path toward dwelling in the gracious Heart of Divine Love.

PERSONAL REFLECTION

How would you define contemplation? In what ways might you enlarge your contemplative vision?

Revisit the description of your heart that you composed at the end of chapter 1. How would you enlarge it? What have you discovered about your own openness of heart?

PERSONAL PRACTICE

Virtues of courage, gratitude, reverence, humility, love, faith, hope, and peace were all folded into this chapter. Pick one of these that speaks to your heart. Ponder ways to increase that virtue as a way to open your heart.

GROUP CONVERSATION

Share ways that you find to be close to God and where God is close to you.

What insights into the open heart have you gained through reading this book and conversing with others? What additional ways might open a person's heart to God's mercy and love?

GROUP ACTION

Craft a "next step" toward cultivating a more open-hearted environment in your home, parish, or broader community. Name at least four or five concrete steps toward doing this.

Heart Warmers

My mother hired Mr. Bigelow to help tend her large garden, and so I often saw him laboring among the gladiolas and roses. As a child, I was wary of his baggy clothes, slouch hat, and stuttering speech. My mother explained the latter by telling me that he suffered "shell shock" while fighting in World War I. This softened my response to him, but I still kept my distance. It wasn't until several years after leaving home that I began to recognize the deep compassion my mother held for the wounds that he carried. I also came to appreciate how she drew Mr. Bigelow into a place of beauty and respite where he could work in quiet solitude and bring his own creativity into the cultivation of a garden. Perhaps the wounding in my mother's life increased the sensitivity she held for a veteran of a violent and bloody war. The sweet memories I retain of the garden were made in part by someone I had no reason to fear and every reason to embrace as a wounded and yet lovable man.

Prayer

EXCERPT FROM "A MEDITATION AT THE FEAST OF SAINT VALENTINE," BY KEN PHILLIPS

O Eternal Beauty,
Grant me the power this day
  to live with thoughtful intention
    in my speech, choices, and actions,
  so that I may build the habit of living gracefully
    and with love
  for the people and experiences that shape my life,
which is Your gift of Love to me each day.

[Pause and breathe in this prayer]

With an open and reverent heart, I pray.
Amen.

FINAL THOUGHTS

"YOU NEED TO TAKE YOUR SOUL SOMEWHERE ELSE." THIS ADVICE WAS OFFERED TO ME YEARS AGO BY A WISE PASTORAL LEADER. It came after I went on a rant about a current event that drew my ire. I draw back to it whenever I get caught up in heart-hardening moments. Those come when we become obsessed or overwhelmed by bad news and unpleasant encounters. Negative experiences adhere immediately in our brains. It is why one rude interaction can wipe out our recollection of an otherwise beautiful day. The result is increased resentment, anger, and potential self-pity. None of these are good for body and soul.

Writing this book took me to a better place. I admit to undertaking it because of the ever-worsening decline in civility and the uptick in cruelty within our institutions of governance and political processes. Retreating to a quiet study room in our local library restored a sense of perspective and balance. I immersed myself in themes of beauty, kindness, respect, mercy, and other virtues that soften and expand the heart. After leaving that space, I was challenged by my own words to hold to these and other virtues and to remain attentive to anything that would give rise to a calloused heart. I can't say I did so perfectly, but the effort has been worth it. Thus, I hope to continue pondering the heartwarming experiences that have enriched my life and to generate the same for others. I continue to find hope in the heart-to-heart encounters that will take our personal and collective souls to someplace better.

...and a few words of thanks

I am ever so grateful to my colleagues at Bayard/Twenty-Third Publications: Dan Smart, David Dziena, Kerry Moriarty, Anne-Louise Mahoney, Michelle Gerstel, and Jeff McCall.

To Linda McCray, Father Bill McNichols, Ken Phillips, Ron Hendricks, and River Woelz for their gifts of creativity and insight.

To the librarians at Salida Regional Library for making space for me to write in peace and quiet.

To my husband, Ron, to whom I dedicated the book and who showed such patience with the time I devoted to the writing of it.

And to my grandchildren, River and Clay, whose joyful exuberance lift my heart each time I am with them.

Heart Warmers

WHAT ENCOUNTER HAVE YOU EXPERIENCED THAT WARMED YOUR HEART? **WRITE ABOUT IT HERE.**

RESOURCES

Books

Boyle, Gregory. *Cherished Belonging: The Healing Power of Love in Divided Times* (Avid Reader Press/Simon & Schuster, 2024).

Bourgeault, Cynthia. *The Wisdom Way of Knowing: Reclaiming an Ancient Tradition to Awaken the Heart* (Jossey-Bass, 2003).

Chodron, Pema. *When Things Fall Apart: Heart Advice for Difficult Times* (Shambhala, 2016).

Godwin, Gail. *Heart: A Natural History of the Heart-Filled Life* (Perennial, 2001).

Harris, Maria. *Dance of the Spirit: The Seven Stages of Women's Spirituality* (Random House Publishing Group, 1991).

Merton, Thomas. *Thoughts in Solitude* (Farrar Straus & Giroux, 1998).

Muller, Wayne. *Learning to Pray: How We Find Heaven on Earth* (Bantam Books, 2003).

Nouwen, Henri. *The Road to Daybreak: A Spiritual Journey* (Image, 1990).

O'Donohue, John. *Anam Cara: A Book of Celtic Wisdom* (HarperCollins, 1997).

O'Donohue, John. *Beauty: Rediscovering the True Sources of Compassion, Serenity, and Hope* (Harper Perennial, 2004).

Remen, Rachel Naomi. *Kitchen Table Wisdom: Stories that Heal* (Riverhead Books, 1997).

Rohlheiser, Ronald. *The Holy Longing* (Doubleday, 1999).

Starr, Mirabai. *The Showings of Julian of Norwich: A New Translation* (Hampton Roads, 2013).

Steindl-Rast, David. *Music of Silence: A Sacred Journey through the Hours of the Day* (Ulysses Press, 1998, 2002).

St. Theresa of Avila. *The Interior Castle*. New Translation and Introduction by Mirabai Starr (Riverhead Books, 2003).

Taylor, Barbara Brown. *An Altar in the World: A Geography of Faith* (HarperOne, 2009).

Teilhard de Chardin, Pierre. *The Heart of Matter* (HarperOne, 2003).

Periodicals and Websites

America: The Jesuit Review
A monthly magazine published by the Jesuits of the United States. It contains news and opinion about Catholicism and how it relates to American politics and cultural life. Available as a print or online subscription. https://www.americamagazine.org/

Center for Action and Contemplation
Daily meditations offered by Father Richard Rohr and others. https://cac.org/daily-meditations

Grateful Living
A website sponsored by the Network for Grateful Living and established by Brother David Steindl-Rast. www.gratefulness.org

RJHendricks Photography
My husband, Ron's, website featuring beautiful images and a display of his extraordinary photographic talent. https://www.rjhendricksphotography.com

Still Blooming
A blog created by my friend and colleague Barbara Radtke and me with reflections on the potential for growth during the second half of life. www.stillblooming.blog

Weavings: A Journal of the Spiritual Life
[Note: This wonderful publication went out of print in 2017. I still have years' worth of back issues and draw upon the wisdom of the authors for insights into various spiritual topics. I hope the reader will explore the works of the authors I have included in the book for further inspiration.] The Upper Room: www.upperroom.org

William Hart McNichols Art Shop
Official website of Father Bill's icons and his blogs. https://frbillmcnichols-sacredimages.com